This book belongs to:

_____

To my little ones, Aria and Link, and to remembering
all of our sleep songs, stories, and adventures.
I cherish the snuggles and the struggles.
They were all moments that I got to share with you. ♥

Copyright © 2021 Kristin Gudenkauf

All rights reserved. No part of this book may be
reproduced or used in any manner without
the prior written permission of the copyright owner,
except for the use of brief quotations in a book review.

To request permission, contact the publisher at
babyrexproductions@gmail.com.

Paperback ISBN: 978-1-7355775-3-1
Hardcover ISBN: 978-1-7355775-4-8
Ebook ISBN: 978-1-7355775-5-5

Written by Kristin Gudenkauf
Illustrated by Camilla Frescura

Printed by Baby Rex Productions, LLC. in the USA.

Baby Rex Productions, LLC.
Tucson, Arizona, USA

How to Snuggle A Wiggly Worm

written by
Kristin Gudenkauf

illustrated by
Camilla Frescura

Have you ever tried to snuggle a worm,

And all they do is **wiggle** and **squirm**?

They move around and around without fail.

Be careful not to hold them
too tight
or they'll wail!
They may pause for just a moment,
But will be writhing again
before you know it.

I know I may sound like a pest,
But how do you settle a worm to rest?

I've tried all sorts of things, but try as I might,
I just can't seem to get it right.

I've tried acting like a plane – arms stretched out wide,

Swooping and Zig-zagging from side to side.

Zooming in and out, around and about.
But the wiggly worm still
wiggles and shouts.

I've acted as captain of a beautiful boat,
One large enough to carry a cow and a goat!
I've **vroom – vroomed** my motorboat engine.

But that didn't work as I had imagined.
I've whooshed the wind to blow up my sail,
But out came those arms
with a whack and a flail.

I conducted a train traveling across the land,
Playing **choo-choo** with my arm and hand.
Telling stories of adventure and a great trip,
Bouncing **chugga** chugga on my hip.

But sleep and rest were not stops along the way,
For a wiggly worm that wanted
more time for play.
Again I ask, if planes, trains, and boats won't do,

How do I snuggle a wiggly worm

for more than a second or two?

I've tried a **toy** as a distraction,

Thinking this time the snuggle will happen!

Try to tire her out with a **puzzle**,

Then a hug from her bear,

Mr. Fuzzle.

We were only a few minutes in,
When the puzzle began to win!

Then puzzle pieces wouldn't sit quite right, she began to have a fit and **fight**.

Streams of tears ran down her cheeks, eyes tired, red, and wide.

Snatching Mr. Fuzzle, she ran away to hide.

I wasn't wrong, there was a snuggle to share,
But it wasn't for me,
it was for the **fuzzy bear**!

So that didn't work, what do I do?
How do I snuggle a wiggly worm
for more than a second or two?

"I've got it!" I said to myself,
Grabbing the flashlight from atop the shelf.
We'll make hand animals and since it's night,
we'll cast shadows on the wall using the light.

We'll lay on the bed,
side by side,
Hands in the air,
fingers stretched wide.

We latched our thumbs and
the butterflies soared.
Pressing fingertips together,
the t-rexes roared.
Octopus fingers whomped and whooshed,
Fishy hands pressed together
swam and swooshed.
This little worm must have
sensed sleep coming fast,
Because the snuggles ended
when the fishy swam past.

I sang,
"You are my sunshine,
my only sunshine,"

She ignored me to play with her toes, then mine!
I sang her favorite songs, every single one.
She made raspberry sounds

- pfffft -
with her tongue.

I sang song after song, verse after verse.

But it only seemed to make things worse.

So, singing helped, but not enough,
Getting a worm to rest sure is tough!
What else can I try?

What more can I do?

How do I snuggle a wiggly worm

for more

than a song

or two?

Books!

That's the trick!

She does love to read.

Books must be the answer to snuggles, indeed!
She handed me one book,
two,
then three.

Then plopped down right next to me.

"The prince rode in",

I read a few pages in,
As her eyes drooped
and began
to dim.

She voiced her disapproval with a **grunt** and a **grumble**.
I thought books would work, but I was wrong.
Not using voices meant snuggles didn't last long.
Why even ask again what one should do,
When a wiggly worm won't snuggle you?

I give up,
I'm the only one sleepy here!

Then, just like that, what did I hear?

I heard the pitter-patter of little feet,
And a sweet voice ask,
"please snuggle me?"
With Mr. Fuzzle and blanket,
arms stretched up high,
I scooped her up in my arms,
teared up,
and sighed.

She didn't need a song or a game,

She didn't need me
but wanted me all the same.

Sleep isn't easy for worms on the go,

But when they are ready
they let you know.

Sweet dreams, wiggly worm,
sleep tight.

I'll snuggle you

all through the night.

Parental Note:

Dear Parents and Caregivers,

As a new mom, I found myself working through new ways to get my little one to sleep every other day. What I found comfort in was having someone remind me to trust my instincts, that struggling does NOT mean I am a bad parent, and sleep will come – eventually.

I had a very special friend, and a specialist, remind me of these things. That's when this book came to me. A fun story with beautiful imagery sharing the truth (at least the truth for some) about the difficulties of just one facet of parenting – getting our little ones to rest.

"How to Snuggle a Wiggly Worm" is a children's book geared toward the family, reminding both parent and child of the ever-changing nature of the roles we play as we grow together. I hope this book helps you smile while thinking back on memories, and I hope the following special note helps you find peace and grace in those moments you feel the struggles of raising a human!

Always yours,
Kristin Gudenkauf (Author)

Note from a Specialist and Veteran Parent:

Sleep plays an integral role in all aspects of our daily life, from allowing our bodies to rest and recover to contributing to physical and mental health challenges. Sleep is essential no matter your age. Newborns to toddlers, teens to grandparents, and everyone in between.

As a registered nurse who suffers from insomnia and had children with sleep issues, How to Snuggle a Wiggly Worm brought back a lot of memories as both a new and veteran parent. Parenting does not come with a manual, nor do babies, toddlers, or teens. There is a learning curve and every child is different. No one way works for every child because they are all different, remind yourself that sleep issues are usually temporary and to TRUST your gut!

You know your child best, you are the parent and therefore get to make whatever decisions you choose to support your parenting philosophy. As an RN, certified postpartum doula, and lactation educator, I have supported and educated thousands of families, both in the hospital and in the home setting and sleep is always a hot topic of discussion. I like to talk to parents-to-be and new parents about HOW they sleep first and HOW much sleep they need to function, then we discuss HOW sleep is going to change for the household once the baby arrives. Setting realistic expectations, being flexible, and giving grace from the beginning can help set them up for success.

Knowing that babies do not have the same sleep cycles as adults do and learning to understand the differences can help parents and caregivers feel more prepared when they are awake sporadically between 1-5 am in the first few weeks.

Developmental milestones, sickness, teething, separation anxiety, nutrition, and a slew of other challenges can also disrupt sleeping patterns. Well-rested kids make for happier kids and happier kids make for happier, well-rested parents.

Having a baby or toddler who does not sleep well, does NOT mean you are a bad parent. Sleep deprivation is hard on everybody and can wreak havoc on a parent's mental health as well. If you have ever suffered or been diagnosed with a mental health disorder, sleep needs to be a priority for you. Napping during the day, asking for help, and taking care of one's self also help make the transition easier. Postpartum depression and anxiety are real (1 in 7 moms and 1 in 10 dads suffer) and are often triggered by a lack of quality sleep.

Help is available and you do not have to go at it alone. Talk with the child's provider if you think something more might be going on. Good-quality sleep is a necessity for everyone. Whether it be a song, a book, a stuffed animal, shadow puppets, or funny voices, cherish the snuggles with your **wiggly worm** for soon they will no longer need that snuggle to fall asleep.

Yours truly,
Colleen Laszakovits

Colleen Laszakovits is an After Baby Consultant, RN, CPD, CLE with Your Family's Journey who provides postpartum and breastfeeding support in Tucson, AZ (www.yourfamilysjourney.com). Additionally, Postpartum Support International provides free and confidential support and resources at 1-800-944-4773 for families needing additional help.

Made in the USA
Columbia, SC
09 October 2021